# Peculiar Plants

## by Robin Twiddy

Minneapolis, Minnesota

## Credits
All images courtesy of Shutterstock. With thanks to Getty Images, Thinkstock Photo, and iStockphoto. Cover and throughout– Ramona Kaulitzki, majcot, Hiba.K.Badr, Toeizuza Thailand, Olkita, Chansom Pantip, illustrator096, Gaidamashchuk, Uglegorets. p4–5 – mikesj11, Purino, MintImages. p6–7 – Gaidamashchuk, Filipe B. Varela, Andrew Massyn, Public domain, via Wikimedia Commons. p8–9 – Vladimir Konstantinov, Peter Yeeles. p10–11 – Dilka Sithari, Darren Kurnia. p12–13 – gg-foto, David Dennis. p14–15 – Vitalii Nesterchuk, I love photo, miya38, Vasin Lee. p16–17 – Medvedeva Oxana, Arnain. p18–19 – Dmitry Demkin, Wantanee Chantasilp. p20–21 – Damsea, boivin nicolas. p22–23 – Michaelnero, anjahennern.

**Bearport Publishing Company Product Development Team**
President: Jen Jenson; Director of Product Development: Spencer Brinker; Managing Editor: Allison Juda; Associate Editor: Naomi Reich; Senior Designer: Colin O'Dea; Associate Designer: Elena Klinkner; Associate Designer: Kayla Eggert; Product Development Specialist: Anita Stasson

*Library of Congress Cataloging-in-Publication Data*

Names: Twiddy, Robin, author.
Title: Peculiar plants / by Robin Twiddy.
Description: Minneapolis, Minnesota : Bearport Publishing Company, [2024] | Series: Can you believe it? | Includes index.
Identifiers: LCCN 2023001971 (print) | LCCN 2023001972 (ebook) | ISBN 9798888220085 (library binding) | ISBN 9798888221945 (paperback) | ISBN 9798888223239 (ebook)
Classification: LCC QK49 .T834 2024  (print) | LCC QK49  (ebook) | DDC 580--dc23
LC record available at https://lccn.loc.gov/2023001971
LC ebook record available at https://lccn.loc.gov/2023001972

© 2024 Booklife Publishing
This edition is published by arrangement with Booklife Publishing.

North American adaptations © 2024 Bearport Publishing Company. All rights reserved. No part of this publication may be reproduced in whole or in part, stored in any retrieval system, or transmitted in any form or by any means, electronic, mechanical, photocopying, recording, or otherwise, without written permission from the publisher.

For more information, write to Bearport Publishing, 5357 Penn Avenue South, Minneapolis, MN 55419.

# Contents

Peculiar Plants...............4
Parts of a Plant .............6
Super Seeds ................8
Fantastic Flowers...........10
Terrific Trees ..............12
Great Grass................14
Remarkable Rain Forests .....16
Dry Deserts ................18
Underwater Wonders........20
Killer Plants...............22
Glossary ..................24
Index ....................24

# Peculiar Plants

There are more than 200,000 kinds of plants all over our planet.

Some are pretty strange. Let's learn about the weirdest plants out there.

# Parts of a Plant

A plant is made of different parts. Each part has a job.

Flowers make seeds.

**Roots** help get water to the plant.

Leaves take in light to help plants grow.

The leaves of a raffia palm tree can be as long as a bowling lane!

# Super Seeds

Seeds travel in interesting ways. Some have tiny hooks that catch on animals' fur.

These horses are carrying burdock seeds.

Harvester ants carry seeds back to their nests as a snack. The parts of seeds that aren't eaten are tossed aside. Then, they grow into new plants.

Ants moving a grass seed

# FANTASTIC Flowers

The Kadupul (KAH-do-pull) flower is not easy to find. This sweet-smelling flower blooms only at night and dies in the morning.

10

Not all flowers smell nice. The corpse flower smells like a dead body. *Pee-yew!*

# TERRIFIC Trees

The rainbow eucalyptus tree looks painted, but it is not. Its **sap** changes colors when it dries.

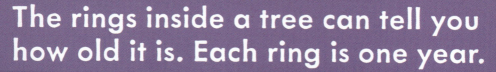

The rings inside a tree can tell you how old it is. Each ring is one year.

13

# GREAT Grass

There are about 12,000 kinds of grasses on Earth.

Wheat

Corn

Rice

Wheat, corn, and rice are grasses that we eat.

14

Bamboo is a grass that grows very quickly.

Some bamboo can grow about 35 inches (90 cm) a day!

# REMARKABLE
# Rain Forests

Many kinds of plants live in the world's rain forests.

16

Rain forests have thick **canopies** at their treetops. There, plants grow very close together. This even slows raindrops falling to the ground.

# DRY Deserts

Cacti can live in dry deserts. A saguaro (suh-WAH-*roh*) cactus can grow to be about 60 feet (18 m) tall.

Cacti stay alive by storing water in their stems. They have spikey **spines** instead of leaves. Spines keep thirsty animals away.

# UNDERWATER Wonders

All plants make **oxygen**, even plants that live underwater. The oxygen from water plants stays in the water.

Seagrass grows underwater.

Giant Amazon water lilies have large leaves that float at the surface. They can be 6 ft (2 m) across.

# KILLER Plants

Some plants can kill. The angel's trumpet flower is **poisonous**. Eating it can stop your heart.

Danger! Do not eat!

Other killer plants eat meat. The pitcher plant traps bugs and small animals. It makes them into a soup to slurp up.

# Glossary

**canopies** the top layers of branches and leaves covering a forest

**oxygen** a gas that animals and people need to live

**poisonous** deadly or dangerous when eaten

**roots** parts of plants that take in water from the ground

**sap** a liquid food found in plants

**spines** hard, sharp growths on some plants

# Index

**animals** 8, 19, 23
**cacti** 18–19
**flowers** 6, 10–11, 22
**leaves** 7, 19, 21
**night** 10
**rings** 13
**seeds** 6, 8–9
**water** 6, 19–21